Original title:
Rising Again

Copyright © 2024 Swan Charm
All rights reserved.

Author: Paulina Pähkel
ISBN HARDBACK: 978-9916-89-850-5
ISBN PAPERBACK: 978-9916-89-851-2
ISBN EBOOK: 978-9916-89-852-9

Celestial Awakening

In the silence, whispers arise,
Heaven's breath in dawn's disguise.
Angels gather, wings unfurled,
To share the grace of a new world.

Stars align in sacred song,
Guiding souls who have wandered long.
With reverence, we lift our plea,
Awake, O spirit, be free.

Branches sway in the gentle breeze,
Nature shares its sacred ease.
The sunlight spills through leafy seams,
Awakening all our hidden dreams.

Faith ignites the heart within,
In every loss, there lies a win.
The path before us shines so bright,
As we follow the guiding light.

Oh, celestial sphere, hold us close,
In your embrace, we find repose.
With gratitude, we seek the way,
To live in hope, come what may.

Heralds of the New Light

From the shadows, a voice does call,
  Ancient wisdom, beckoning all.
  New beginnings break the night,
  Heralds rise, proclaiming light.

Hands uplifted toward the sky,
  We are one, we cannot deny.
Through trials faced, our spirits soar,
  Together we stand, forevermore.

In the stillness, hearts will mend,
  With every prayer, we transcend.
  The dawn awakens hope anew,
In each soul, the light shines through.

Mountains echo our sweet refrain,
In love's embrace, we feel no pain.
With every step, we pave the way,
To share our truths in bright array.

Praise the morning, the canvas clear,
  With open hearts, we gather here.
  Heralds of joy, let voices ring,
    In the light of love, we sing.

The Lifting of Veils

In silence, we gather, a whisper of grace,
The veils of the world, in soft light, we trace.
Hearts open wide to the sacred embrace,
As shadows recede, divinity's face.

With eyes turned to heavens, in prayer we align,
The truths of the spirit, in chorus, we find.
Each moment a gift, each breath, a design,
In the lifting of veils, our souls intertwine.

Rejoicing in the Spirit

Lift up your voices, let praises arise,
In the dance of the spirit, our hopes touch the skies.
With joy overflowing, like rivers we flow,
In the warmth of His love, our hearts brightly glow.

In every heartbeat, a rhythm divine,
The laughter of angels, in harmony shine.
Together we stand, in the promise of time,
Rejoicing in light, our spirits entwined.

Ascension of the Heart

With each sacred step, our spirits ascend,
To the heights of His love, where all sorrows end.
A journey of grace, where pain turns to art,
In the quiet communion, the ascension of heart.

Through trials we wander, yet faith lights the way,
In the arms of compassion, we gather each day.
Our lives, a reflection of His love's part,
In the stillness of being, the ascension of heart.

A Symphony of Hope

Hear the echoes of faith, a symphony pure,
In each note of despair, a promise is sure.
As melodies mingle with dreams yet to grow,
Together we rise in this symphony of hope.

In the tapestry woven, our stories entwine,
With threads of compassion, like stars that align.
Through valleys of shadow, we sing and we cope,
In the heart of the struggle, a symphony of hope.

Glistening in Grace

In the light of dawn's embrace,
We rise to seek Your face.
Heavenly whispers call us near,
In Your arms, we lose our fear.

Joyful hearts, we sing in praise,
Boundless love through endless days.
Each moment shines with truth divine,
In Your gaze, our spirits shine.

Unbroken Chains

Chains of sorrow, cast away,
In Your strength, we find our way.
No more burdens, no more strife,
You have given us new life.

Every tear, a seed of grace,
Turning darkness into space.
Freedom flows, like rivers wide,
In Your love, we now abide.

Steps of the Redeemer

With each step, we follow You,
Guided by the path so true.
Footprints marked in dust and pain,
Lead us through the joy and rain.

In the silence, hear Your call,
Lift us high, lest we should fall.
Through the valleys, through the night,
Hand in hand, You are our light.

Redemption's Path

On this road, redemption gleams,
Like a tapestry of dreams.
With each mile, our hearts grow bold,
In Your promise, we behold.

Guide us softly, day by day,
As we walk, our fears give way.
In Your mercy, we are free,
On this path, You walk with me.

Blessings of Reconstruction

In the ruins of despair, hope remains,
Brick by brick, we rise to heal the pains.
With hands united, we build anew,
A sanctuary of faith, where love shines through.

Each fracture tells a story, whispered low,
Of strength found deep in the heart's warm glow.
The past, though heavy, does not define,
The canvas of tomorrow, love intertwines.

Through trials we find the grace to see,
In every shadow, a possibility.
We gather stones, to pave the way,
For brighter tomorrows, in the light of day.

With every prayer, the walls take shape,
In sacred spaces, our spirits escape.
From ashes we rise, renewed by the light,
In the blessings of reconstruction, we find our might.

The Promise of Dawn

In the stillness of night, whispers call,
The stars are guides, on darkness we stall.
Yet in silence, a promise awaits,
A new day to rise, as hope celebrates.

With every heartbeat, the shadows retreat,
The dawn brings warmth, the night feels complete.
Golden rays spill on the dewy grass,
As souls awaken, let worries pass.

With faith we embark, on this journey wide,
In the light of truth, we shall abide.
Each moment a gift, a chance to renew,
The promise of dawn paints our skies blue.

Hope like a river, flows ever strong,
It carries our spirits, in a joyful song.
With open hearts, we embrace the morn,
In the promise of dawn, all fears are scorned.

Ascending Through Struggles

Upon the mountains, shadows loom large,
Yet the spirit whispers, 'Take heart, take charge.'
With courage as armor, we climb so high,
Through trials and storms, our spirits will fly.

Each stone on the path, a lesson learned,\nIn the fire of struggle, our souls are turned.
Faith is our compass, guiding us through,
In the ascent of our lives, we start anew.

With every heartbeat, resilience ignites,
The promise of strength in the darkest nights.
For every wound, there's a chance to grow,
In the dance of life, we learn to flow.

Together we rise, hand in hand we soar,
Through the valleys of doubt, we reach for more.
Ascending through struggles, we form our bond,
In the light of love's embrace, we respond.

Eclipsed No More

In the shadows, where silence dwells,
We break the chains of haunting spells.
No longer hidden, we vow to be free,
In the light of truth, our spirits agree.

With every moment, the dawn draws near,
No longer eclipsed, we let go of fear.
In unity's strength, we shatter the dark,
Igniting within, a passionate spark.

Hope like a beacon, shines brightly ahead,
Guided by faith, on mercy we tread.
With love as our compass, we voyage anew,
To worlds unexplored, where dreams come true.

As we cast off the veils of despair,
The light of the heavens flows in the air.
Eclipsed no more, in love we embrace,
The radiant journey, our sacred space.

A New Covenant

In shadows cast, the light will break,
A promise forged in timeless grace.
Hearts renewed, in love awoke,
A sacred bond we now embrace.

From ashes rise, the faithful sing,
With every tear, redemption found.
The Almighty's hand, a guiding wing,
In unity, forever bound.

Wanderers lost in sin and strife,
Shall find their way, the path is clear.
A covenant of endless life,
With hope restored, we draw near.

The stone is rolled, the veil is torn,
In every heart, His Spirit flows.
New beginnings, each day is born,
With grace that in our being grows.

Together we will stand as one,
In love's embrace, we'll seek our fate.
The journey starts with faith begun,
In His great light, we celebrate.

Embracing the Divine

In quiet moments, still we pray,
The whispers of the heart align.
Through every trial, come what may,
We seek, oh Lord, Your light so fine.

With open arms, we welcome grace,
In every dawn, a chance to bloom.
In sacred space, we seek Your face,
Your love dispels the deepest gloom.

As rivers flow, Your mercy pours,
Awakening the weary soul.
In faith, we walk through heaven's doors,
In unity, we are made whole.

Through every storm, our spirits rise,
With steadfast hearts, we hold the flame.
In Your vast love, we find our prize,
To You, O Lord, we lift Your name.

With gratitude, we sing each day,
For in Your arms, we find our peace.
In every trial, we choose to stay,
Embracing You, our joys increase.

Flourishing After Tribulation

In trials faced, the heart is stirred,
Through darkest nights, our souls will grow.
Each tear that's shed, a silent word,
In faith, we nurture what we sow.

From barren lands, the flowers rise,
In every storm, a lesson learned.
Through pain and loss, our spirits prize,
A brighter day, our hearts discerned.

With every step, our hope ignites,
In desert winds, we seek the rain.
The path ahead, with sacred lights,
Transforming loss into the gain.

When shadows linger, we won't fear,
For in the struggle, strength is found.
With each new dawn, the sky is clear,
In sacred woods, our roots are bound.

So let us dance in joy and praise,
For life is but a fleeting breath.
In faith, we find the hidden ways,
Flourishing, transcending death.

Sacred Revival

Awake, O hearts, from slumber deep,
In sacred fire, our spirits rise.
The promise made, a truth we keep,
Reviving souls beneath the skies.

From quiet woods to mountains grand,
In every whisper, nature calls.
Together, joined, we take a stand,
In faith's embrace, our spirit sprawls.

In every song, His love resounds,
Through every tear, the healing flows.
In sacred circles, grace abounds,
As light within us ever grows.

With joyful hearts, we seek the light,
Through darkest night, the dawn will break.
In love's embrace, we find our sight,
In service pure, our path we make.

In harmony, we rise and sing,
A chorus joined, both vast and wide.
For in this life, we are the spring,
A sacred revival, love our guide.

The Promise of Tomorrow

In shadows cast, the light will break,
A whisper soft, the dawn awakes.
With faith we rise, from ashes free,
To claim the hope, we yearn to see.

The stars above, in heaven's grace,
Guide weary hearts to a sacred place.
Through trials faced and burdens borne,
We find our path, in grace reborn.

Each step we take, a promise true,
In every tear, a chance anew.
The heavens sing, their voices blend,
In love's embrace, we shall transcend.

The morning sun, like balm, restores,
The weary soul, forever soars.
In every struggle, find your way,
Embrace the light, it's here to stay.

The promise dwells in every heart,
With strength renewed, we'll never part.
For in our faith, tomorrow shines,
In every moment, love entwines.

Celestial Renewal

The moonlight bathes the earth so bright,
As stars awaken in the night.
In silent prayer, we seek the dawn,
In gentle whispers, hope is drawn.

With each new breath, the spirit stirs,
In harmony, the universe purrs.
The sacred dance of life unfolds,
In nature's arms, the truth enfolds.

Like rivers flow, the seasons change,
A cosmic cycle, vast and strange.
We shed our past, like autumn leaves,
In every ending, new life weaves.

The heavens call, they urge us near,
In stillness deep, we face our fear.
Divine embrace, a light within,
We rise anew, as hearts begin.

Through storms we walk, our spirits bright,
With faith as guide, we seek the light.
Celestial songs can heal the soul,
In every heart, we find our role.

Phoenix of the Soul

From ashes deep, the spirit flies,
A flame ignites, beneath the skies.
With every wound, a story told,
The heart transforms, in strength so bold.

In twilight's glow, we shed our skin,
The fire burns away the sin.
Like phoenix rise, from depths of night,
In brilliant hues, we take to flight.

The trials faced, our guiding hand,
In love's embrace, together stand.
With wings outstretched, we break the mold,
Our souls united, brave and bold.

In sacred rites, we find our breath,
For every end be but a step.
The journey vast, the light our thread,
In faith we trust, the past is shed.

Together we soar, with spirits high,
On wings of love, we touch the sky.
The phoenix sings, a sacred vow,
In every heart, we rise somehow.

Hymn of New Beginnings

In morning's light, we find our way,
With hope renewed, we greet the day.
Each moment fresh, a sacred gift,
In rivers clear, our spirits lift.

With open hearts, we seek the truth,
In every laughter, echoes youth.
The past we honor, but let it go,
For in the now, our spirits flow.

We gather strength, from souls once lost,
To rise again, despite the cost.
The hymn begins, in harmony,
In unity, we find the key.

With every dawn, the promise grows,
In whispered prayers, our purpose flows.
Each step we take, a leap of faith,
In love's embrace, we find our grace.

Embrace the new, the chance to bloom,
For every heart can conquer gloom.
A hymn of hope, a song we sing,
In every soul, new life takes wing.

The Gift of Renewal

In quiet moments, grace descends,
A whisper soft, the heart it mends.
With every dawn, a promise stays,
To guide our steps in ancient ways.

Beneath the shadows, light does bloom,
In sacred spaces, casting gloom.
The spirit rises, free to soar,
Reborn in love, forevermore.

Through trials faced, we find our peace,
In faith, the burdens find release.
With every tear, a seed is sown,
A testament of love, we've grown.

The world may storm, yet we stand firm,
In every heart, a gentle term.
Embrace the change, the cycle's spin,
For in the loss, new life begins.

Shattered Chains

In darkest hours, we call your name,
With faith unyielding, we reclaim.
Chains that bind, now fall away,
In holy light, we find our way.

With every breath, a freeing song,
We rise united, brave and strong.
No more the past, we journey on,
Awake to love, the night is gone.

The chains of doubt, no longer hold,
In your embrace, the heart made bold.
From ashes rise, our spirits bright,
In freedom's glow, we seek the light.

Together we stand, hand in hand,
In sacred bonds, forever planned.
With courage found, we face the day,
In your presence, fear gives way.

Beyond the Ruins

In fallen cities, hope remains,
A whisper soft through shattered pains.
From rubble's dust, new dreams take flight,
In hearts ablaze, igniting light.

The past may haunt, but can't define,
What lies ahead, a chance divine.
With every step, we build again,
A future bright, where love won't end.

Beyond the ruins, beauty grows,
In fertile ground, a garden flows.
From ashes rise, the brave and bold,
In sacred truths, a tale retold.

With faith as guide, we forge the way,
In unity, we find our say.
Though storms may rage, our hearts unite,
Beyond the ruins, we find the light.

Radiance in the Storm

When tempests howl and shadows creep,
Your light, O Lord, brings peace so deep.
In fierce winds that threaten to sway,
We seek your calm to guide our way.

Amidst the storm, your whispers flow,
A gentle breeze, where hope will grow.
In trials faced, we stand as one,
With hearts ablaze, till battle's won.

The rain may fall, the thunder roar,
Yet in our souls, your strength restores.
From darkest nights, we rise anew,
With faith and trust, we journey through.

In every trial, your hand we find,
A loving touch, forever kind.
Through storms we walk, with spirits warm,
In radiance, we find our form.

A Pathway to Paradise

In stillness find the way,
Where shadows bow to light,
With faith, we walk each day,
Embracing love's pure sight.

The journey stretches wide,
With blessings as our guide,
Each step a sacred stride,
In grace, we shall abide.

The whispers of the trees,
Tell tales of ancient lore,
In harmony, we seize,
The promise of much more.

Through valleys dark and deep,
We seek the holy flame,
In prayers, our souls will leap,
To glorify His name.

A pathway paved with tears,
Transforms to streams of gold,
In love that calms our fears,
A truth that must be told.

Reflections of the Divine

In silence, hearts unite,
With visions soft and clear,
We gather in His light,
In faith, we draw Him near.

The heavens sing His song,
With echoes pure and bright,
In every note, we long,
To bask in endless light.

Each leaf a voice of grace,
A mirror to the soul,
In nature's sweet embrace,
We find our holy goal.

Through trials, we ascend,
With courage as our shield,
In love, our hearts will mend,
In truth, our fate is sealed.

Reflections in our eyes,
Reveal the sacred thread,
With faith, we rise and rise,
To where the angels tread.

The Second Wind of Grace

When burdens weigh us down,
And hope begins to fade,
We seek a higher crown,
In grace, our fears allayed.

With gentle breath renewed,
We stand upon the brink,
In gratitude, imbued,
We find the strength to think.

The trials we have faced,
Are lessons carved in stone,
In every tear, a trace,
Of love that we have grown.

The dawn breaks crisp and clear,
With whispers of the morn,
In faith, we have no fear,
From ashes, we are born.

In every moment's grace,
A second chance we see,
To rise and find our place,
In perfect unity.

A Tapestry of Hope

With threads of love entwined,
A tapestry unfurls,
In every heart, aligned,
We weave the light that swirls.

Through colors bright and bold,
Each story has its part,
In unity, we're told,
The journey of the heart.

With every gentle hand,
We stitch the dreams we share,
In faith, together stand,
With strength born from our care.

The fibers tell our tale,
Of struggles, peace, and strife,
In each, a sacred veil,
The essence of our life.

So let the weaver's grace,
Embrace us as we strive,
In hope, our hearts will chase,
A love that helps us thrive.

The Light beyond the Storm

In shadows deep, His love shines bright,
A beacon strong, through darkest night.
With every tear, He wipes away,
In faith, we find our guiding way.

The storms may rage, the winds may howl,
Yet still we trust, we humbly bow.
For in the tempest, He draws near,
His whisper calm, dispels our fear.

Through trials grand, our hearts of gold,
With every challenge, His truth unfolds.
We stand, resilient, hand in hand,
Embraced by grace, forever stand.

The dawn will break, our eyes will see,
A world reborn, in unity.
With every heartbeat, we proclaim,
The Light will lead us, in His name.

So let us journey, brave and free,
Through every struggle, we will see.
The Light beyond, forever warm,
Our souls transformed, through every storm.

New Horizons of Grace

Upon the dawn, new mercies bloom,
Awakening hearts to love's sweet tune.
With every step, His hand we seek,
In whispers soft, He makes us weak.

The mountains rise, yet faith will scale,
With hope as anchor, we shall not fail.
In valleys low, His promise stands,
A gentle guide, through shifting sands.

Through every trial, grace unfolds,
Like precious jewels, His truth beholds.
With eyes of faith, we see the way,
New horizons greet the breaking day.

As rivers flow and seasons change,
His love remains, though times feel strange.
In every sorrow, joy will chase,
We find our strength in His embrace.

So let us soar, on wings of prayer,
Embracing love, beyond compare.
With open hearts, we'll dance and sing,
New horizons, joy they bring.

Ascending Faithfully

With every step, the path is clear,
In faith we rise, dispelling fear.
The heavens call, our spirits soar,
In unity, we seek the shore.

The trials faced, like mountains tall,
We climb with grace, we will not fall.
His light awaits, above the fray,
In love's embrace, we find our way.

Each prayer we lift, a gentle breeze,
Bringing us hope, our hearts at ease.
The journey long, yet ever true,
With steadfast hearts, we press on through.

In sacred space, we sit in peace,
From earthly burdens, our souls release.
Through stormy nights and blazing days,
Ascending high, we sing His praise.

So let us rise, with hearts ablaze,
In every moment, seek His ways.
With faithful steps, together bound,
Ascending faithfully, joy is found.

Journey to the Infinite

With every breath, the journey starts,
A sacred quest that stirs our hearts.
Through valleys low and peaks so high,
We seek the truth that will not die.

In stillness deep, His voice we hear,
Guiding our souls, dispelling fear.
Through every road, and twist of fate,
Embraced by grace, we contemplate.

The stars that shine, a glimpse above,
Remind us of His endless love.
A tapestry of life unfolds,
In threads of faith, our story holds.

As time unravels, seasons blend,
We find our way, as we ascend.
Each moment cherished, a gift divine,
Journey to the Infinite, we entwine.

So let us walk, hand in hand as one,
Beneath the moon, beneath the sun.
The journey vast, yet close we stay,
In love's embrace, we'll find our way.

Unbroken Threads of Faith

In quiet moments, prayers arise,
Threads of hope reach for the skies.
Hearts entwined, we stand as one,
In His light, our battles won.

Through trials faced and shadows cast,
The flame of faith will ever last.
Each whisper heard, a guiding hand,
In every storm, we make our stand.

With every heartbeat, love does flow,
A tapestry of grace we'll sew.
In every tear, a promise sown,
In sacred trust, we are not alone.

Through valleys deep and mountains high,
We lift our gaze, our spirits fly.
With courage found in sacred ground,
In His embrace, our peace is found.

The unbroken threads of faith remain,
In unity, we share the gain.
Together walking, hand in hand,
To spread His word across the land.

Miracles of the Morning

The dawn awakens, light unfolds,
In every moment, truth behold.
Soft whispers dance on gentle breeze,
In nature's arms, our souls find ease.

The sun ascends with golden grace,
A sacred touch, a warm embrace.
Each dewdrop glistens, pure and bright,
A testament of morning light.

With faith renewed, the heart takes flight,
In each new day, His love ignites.
The world, adorned in colors rare,
Miracles abound in morning air.

The songbirds call, a joyous sound,
In every heartbeat, grace is found.
With open eyes, we see the signs,
Of heavenly gifts, His love defines.

In every breath, a chance to see,
The miracles setting us free.
Together we rise, ready to sing,
Praising the dawn that each day brings.

The Sacred Transformation

In shadows deep, the heart is stirred,
Through trials faced, His voice is heard.
A journey marked by grace and tears,
He leads us through our greatest fears.

From ashes rise, the soul reborn,
In faith's embrace, we are adorned.
The chains that bind begin to break,
With every step, our spirits wake.

The river flows, a stream divine,
Washing over, His love will shine.
In sacred waters, life awakens,
Old wounds healed, new paths are taken.

With open hearts, we seek the change,
From brokenness, we find exchange.
In Holy light, our doubts dissolve,
In His embrace, our fears resolve.

The sacred transformation sings,
A melody of hope it brings.
In unity, we rise as one,
Forever changed, our hearts are won.

Paths of the Redeemed

Upon the road where faith leads on,
The paths of the redeemed are drawn.
In every step, His love avowed,
Through trials faced, we stand so proud.

With open hearts, we walk in grace,
Hand in hand, we seek His face.
In kindness shown, His light will gleam,
Together, we fulfill the dream.

In whispers soft, He guides our way,
In every dawn, a brand new day.
The lessons learned in love so pure,
In paths of faith, our souls endure.

With every heartbeat, truth prevails,
In service given, love never fails.
Through victories small and battles grand,
United in His guiding hand.

In paths of the redeemed, we find,
A legacy of love intertwined.
With grateful hearts, we sing His praise,
In endless joy, our spirits raise.

Lifting the Veil of Night

In the stillness, stars align,
A whisper stirs the holy air,
Guiding souls to light divine,
Awakening hearts from despair.

Morning sun breaks the gray sky,
Casting hope across the land,
Lost in shadows, dreams still fly,
With faith, together we stand.

Each hymn sung, a sacred prayer,
Resounding through the earth's embrace,
In the dark, we find our care,
Lifting burdens with grace.

Voices rise with pure intent,
Echoing through valley wide,
In our hearts, the flame is lent,
Guiding all who seek and bide.

With every dawn, a new decree,
The veil of night begins to fade,
In unity, we shall be free,
In love, our spirits will cascade.

The Silent Choir of Change

In the quiet, whispers swell,
Nature sings a softer tune,
Each leaf, a tale it has to tell,
Dance of dusk, the rise of moon.

Fractured shadows mend and weave,
While stars break into shimmering light,
In still waters, we believe,
Guided gently, hearts take flight.

The earth, it turns with sacred grace,
Transforming wounds into the whole,
In every breath, we find our place,
The silent choir calls the soul.

A sacred promise lingers near,
As seasons shift and time unfolds,
With every pulse, we feel no fear,
In life's embrace, the truth beholds.

Through quiet storms, we find our way,
A symphony of hearts unite,
Together, we shall always stay,
In love's warm glow, we ignite.

Emblems of the Everlasting

In the garden, faith does bloom,
Petals brush against the sky,
Each symbol sheds its earthly gloom,
Binding us to love's reply.

Through the ages, wisdom grows,
Roots entwined in sacred ground,
With every trial, our spirit knows,
In silence, holy truths abound.

The dawn reflects a timeless grace,
Emblems worn through troubled days,
In this sacred, sacred space,
Our hearts sing of endless ways.

Mountains rise, their strength bestowed,
Beneath the weight of stars' caress,
In the journey, love bestowed,
Guides the lost with tenderness.

As we gather, hands entwined,
United in a sacred quest,
In the heart, the truth defined,
Emblems of life, eternally blessed.

Awakening from Shadows

From the depths, voices emerge,
A chorus shaped by time's own hand,
Beneath the weight of night's vast surge,
Hope ignites, a guiding strand.

Light breaks softly, a gentle balm,
Wiping tears from weary eyes,
In the stillness, we find our calm,
A tender prayer beneath the skies.

Each heartbeat pulses with the dawn,
Awakening dreams once held tight,
In the promise of what's reborn,
Shadows flee, succumbing to light.

Through the dark, our spirits soar,
With every step, the chains set free,
Carrying love forevermore,
Awakening to what can be.

In the journey, we find our way,
Guided by faith's gentle hand,
Emerging from night into day,
Together, as one, we shall stand.

Light Through the Veil

In shadows cast, the light will break,
Divine whispers through silence wake.
A path unveiled, as faith ignites,
Guiding souls to heavenly heights.

Through trials faced, we find our grace,
In every tear, the Savior's face.
Hope's soft glow in darkest night,
Reveals the truth, our hearts take flight.

With every prayer, a bridge is built,
From earthly pain, to love distilled.
Every heartbeat knows the call,
To rise above, to stand so tall.

The light descends, it breaks the chains,
Transforming loss to sacred gains.
In unity, we find our way,
As dawn unfolds, it leads to day.

With faith as compass, love our sail,
We journey on, through every gale.
The veil is thin, the promise near,
In light we walk, without the fear.

Blossoms from the Ruins

From ashes gray, new life will spring,
In brokenness, our voices sing.
The ruins tell of battles fought,
Yet from them rise the dreams we sought.

In every crack, a story dwells,
Of hope reborn, where courage swells.
The heart stands firm, though storms may roar,
In desolation, faith restores.

Each petal soft, with colors bright,
Reflects the struggle, finds the light.
In sacred earth, our roots go deep,
Awakening love, in silence, we reap.

Through darkest nights, the stars will gleam,
In every tear, a sacred dream.
Resilience blooms, a fragrant gift,
In every heart, God's spirit lifts.

With open arms, we brave the storm,
In every loss, new life is born.
Through trials faced, the beauty grows,
In ruins strong, the heart bestows.

Spirit's Ascent

With wings of hope, the spirit soars,
Through skies of grace, the heart implores.
Each whispered prayer, a gentle guide,
In every trial, we turn inside.

The mountain high, the valley low,
In every step, our spirits flow.
Ascend with trust, let burdens fall,
In sacred silence, answer the call.

The sacred flame, within us burns,
With every lesson, the spirit learns.
In faith we rise, beyond the pain,
Through love's embrace, we break the chain.

In unity, our souls align,
On paths of light, through grace we climb.
Each heartbeat echoes, the spirit's plea,
In every moment, we seek to be.

The journey long, the way unknown,
Yet in each heart, seeds of grace are sown.
With steadfast love, we seek the heights,
Together bound, to share the light.

Tapestry of Reclamation

In threads of loss, a pattern we weave,
Reclaiming light, in what we believe.
Each moment stitched, with love's embrace,
In every tear, a sacred space.

From darkest nights, the dawn will rise,
Together woven, beneath the skies.
Each strand of hope, a tale retold,
In every heart, a spark of gold.

With hands of grace, we mend the seams,
Restoring beauty to shattered dreams.
The colors blend, a vibrant hue,
In unity, we start anew.

Embracing all, both joy and pain,
In every stitch, love's truth remains.
Through trials faced, the hearts reclaim,
A tapestry, not just a name.

With love as thread, we shape our fate,
In every life, God's love translates.
From ashes rise, a masterpiece,
In this grand weave, we find our peace.

Whispers of Renewal

In quiet prayers, the spirit flows,
Each gentle breeze, a promise grows.
From deep within, the heart will sing,
A song of love, to all we cling.

The rivers cleanse, the mountains rise,
Beneath the heavens, our faith flies.
New dawn shall break, a path revealed,
In sacred trust, our wounds are healed.

With every tear, a seed is sown,
A garden blooms where once was stone.
The sun descends, embracing night,
Yet in the dark, we find our light.

The hands of grace, they lift us high,
To dance among the stars that lie.
The whispers soft, they guide our way,
A testament to the new day.

Let every soul, come forth to see,
The whispered love that sets us free.
And in our hearts, let faith ignite,
For renewal springs from purest light.

The Dawn of Hope

In darkness deep, a flicker glows,
A promise soft the morning shows.
With every breath, our spirits soar,
The dawn of hope forevermore.

From shadows cast, we rise anew,
With hands outstretched, the light breaks through.
Each step we take, a bridge we build,
In sacred trust, our fears are stilled.

The songs of angels fill the air,
Reminding us that love is fair.
With hearts aligned, we seek the grace,
To find our truth in every place.

With faith as strong as mountains stand,
Together guided by His hand.
The dawn shall lift our weary eyes,
To glimpse the hope that never dies.

Let every soul embrace the morn,
With joy reborn, our hearts adorned.
And in this light, we shall arise,
The dawn of hope, our greatest prize.

From Ashes to Glory

In the fire's wake, we gather round,
From ashes lost, new strength is found.
With hearts aflame, we rise anew,
Embracing dreams, our souls break through.

The trials faced, they shape our light,
In darkest moments, we find our might.
Forged in the flames, our spirits grow,
From ashes deep, our faith will flow.

Through every storm, a lesson learned,
In every struggle, our hearts have yearned.
To lift each other, hand in hand,
United strong, together stand.

The path ahead, though steep and long,
Will lead us forth where we belong.
From ashes rise to heights untold,
In glory's light, our hearts unfold.

Let every wound be healed with grace,
As we embrace this sacred space.
Together, we'll ascend the hill,
From ashes to glory, we shall fulfill.

Embracing the Light

When shadows fall and hopes seem dim,
We turn our eyes and grow within.
To seek the light, our hearts ignite,
In deepest night, we find what's right.

With every step, the dawn draws near,
To guide us on, dispelling fear.
In unity, our spirits blend,
Embracing light, our souls transcend.

Through trials faced, the path we tread,
Each burdens lifted, gently spread.
With every dawn, we shall rejoice,
Together strong, we find our voice.

The love divine shines ever bright,
Illuminating our darkest night.
With hearts made pure, we rise above,
Embracing light, embracing love.

Let every soul, be free to see,
The light within, our destiny.
In harmony, we shall unite,
For we are one, embracing light.

From Darkness to Dawn

In shadows deep where silence dwells,
A whispered prayer, the heart compels.
From weary night, the soul takes flight,
To greet the dawn, reclaim the light.

With every tear, a lesson learned,
Through trials faced, the spirit burned.
In faith we rise, from earth to sky,
Our hopes reborn, and fears must die.

The stars above, a guiding grace,
Through darkest paths, in love's embrace.
We walk the road, hand in hand,
For in His name, together we stand.

From ashes gray, to colors bright,
We seek the truth, we chase the light.
In every heart, a flame ignites,
For dawn will come, as day ignites.

In silent prayer, we trust the way,
For every night gives way to day.
Awake, arise, in joy we sing,
The gift of life, our offering.

Beacons of Hope

In every heart, a spark divine,
A light that shines, a love, a sign.
When shadows loom, and fears surround,
We lift our eyes, His grace abound.

Through stormy seas, our faith will sail,
In darkest hours, we shall not fail.
Each whispered prayer, a guiding star,
With courage bright, we journey far.

Together bound, in love's sweet grace,
We find our path, we seek His face.
With open hands, we share the flame,
In every heart, we praise His name.

When hope seems lost, remember this,
His gentle hand is not amiss.
For in our struggles, strength is found,
A beacon bright, where love abounds.

With every dawn, there comes anew,
The promise strong, His word is true.
So let us rise, let spirits soar,
The light of hope forevermore.

Resilient Spirit

In trials faced, the spirit grows,
A river strong, through ebb and flow.
With courage fierce, we stand our ground,
In faith and love, our strength is found.

When tempests rage and shadows fall,
We lift our hearts, and heed the call.
For in the storm, His voice we hear,
Our path unveiled, we cast out fear.

Each scar we bear, a story told,
Of battles won, and hearts of gold.
Through every storm, we rise anew,
As phoenix flames, our light breaks through.

In unity, we walk as one,
With hearts ablaze, till day is done.
The sun will shine, with strength bestowed,
Together we shall walk the road.

So onward brave, with spirits high,
His love our guide, we shall not die.
For in His grace, our souls abide,
A resilient spirit, everwide.

The Resurrection of Dreams

In whispered hopes, the heart will sigh,
As dreams once lost begin to fly.
With open hands, we lift our plight,
In faith, we trust, our dreams ignite.

Through valleys low, and mountains grand,
We seek the spark, His guiding hand.
With every step, the path unfolds,
A story new, in faith retold.

From ashes deep, rebirth will rise,
To greet the dawn, all fears despise.
With every tear, a seed we sow,
In love's pure light, our spirits grow.

Remember this, as shadows fade,
The dreams we chase, will never jade.
In every heart, a song remains,
Of hope restored, through joy and pain.

So let us dream, and dream anew,
With every breath, His love our cue.
In unity, our spirits beam,
Together rise, the resurrection of dreams.

Transcendent Resurgence

In shadows deep, a whisper calls,
A spark ignites, breaking the walls.
Heaven's grace, a gentle breeze,
Lifts our hearts, sets us at ease.

Through trials faced, we find our way,
In darkest nights, we see the day.
With every tear, redemption shows,
The path of love, it gently flows.

Eternal light, our guiding star,
Drawn closer still, no matter how far.
In faith we rise, through pain we soar,
Reborn in spirit, forever more.

The weary soul finds rest tonight,
In arms of hope, a pure delight.
No longer lost, in truth we stand,
Together bound, in love's own hand.

So lift your voice, in joyful song,
For in our hearts, we all belong.
A transcendent tune, a chorus bright,
We march as one toward the light.

Renewed in Faith

Upon the hills, the dawn breaks free,
A promise made, for you and me.
With every breath, we seek the grace,
To find our truth, in love's embrace.

The storms may roar, the winds may howl,
Yet in our hearts, we feel the vow.
For hope is here, amidst the fight,
Renewed in faith, we find our light.

Through valleys low, the shadows may creep,
But in His name, our souls will leap.
With every prayer, we soar above,
Bound tightly in His endless love.

The past is washed, the future bright,
Our hearts are whole, made pure and right.
Together strong, we rise anew,
In every step, we walk in truth.

So lift your gaze, let Spirit shine,
Trust in the path that is divine.
Renewed in faith, we claim our place,
In unity, we find our grace.

The Return of Light

When darkness seemed to rule the hour,
A glimmer glows, a sacred power.
From depths of night, we hear Him call,
The return of light, it breaks the fall.

With every heart that dares to seek,
In quiet whispers, the soul will speak.
His radiance spreads, like morning's kiss,
Turning our tears to boundless bliss.

The chains of doubt start to release,
In arms of love, we find our peace.
The shadows flee, the dawn draws near,
In every moment, His voice we hear.

So let us rise, with hands held tight,
Embracing truth, and all things bright.
In unity, we spread His flame,
The world transformed, forever changed.

Dance in the glory, sing in the day,
For in His light, we find our way.
The return of light, a wondrous sight,
Together, we shine, pure and bright.

Ascending from Ashes

From ashes cold, we rise again,
In whispered prayers, we break the chain.
With every hurt, we find our song,
Together, in love, we all belong.

The embers glow, a flicker bright,
In darkest times, we seek the light.
Through trials fierce, our spirits blend,
In unity, we will not bend.

Like phoenix born from flames so high,
In grace we soar, we touch the sky.
With every step, our voices blend,
Each heart a note, love knows no end.

Let fears be gone, let courage lead,
In every act, in word and deed.
From ashes fine, we bloom anew,
With faith as roots, our souls break through.

So rise, dear friends, in hope and cheer,
For in our hearts, the truth is clear.
Ascending from ashes, we will be,
A living testament, wild and free.

Light's Return

In darkness deep, we sought the dawn,
A whisper soft, the night withdrawn.
The rays of hope, like golden tide,
In every heart, they now abide.

With gentle hands, He guides the way,
Through shadows cast, we find our sway.
The sun anew, with fervent grace,
Illuminates our weary face.

His love's embrace, a sacred beam,
Awakens life, ignites the dream.
In every moment, pure and bright,
We stand united, in His light.

The path is clear, the veil now torn,
With every step, our souls reborn.
The journey long, but faith holds true,
For in His warmth, we start anew.

So let us rise, and sing His praise,
For in His arms, our spirits blaze.
With hearts on fire, we now discern,
The sacred glow, our light's return.

Emancipation of the Soul

From chains that bind, we turn and plead,
Awakening the heart's deep seed.
In silent cries, our spirits long,
To break the night and sing the song.

A fervent prayer comes from within,
To find the peace that conquers sin.
Each breath a step, toward freedom's grace,
In His embrace, we find our place.

With every burden cast aside,
The weight of worlds, we now abide.
The chains of fear, they fall away,
In faith's embrace, we greet the day.

Eternal light shall guide our quest,
Anointed souls, forever blessed.
With lifted hands, we break the night,
In unity, we rise to fight.

So dance, rejoice, for we are whole,
In love's sweet name, we claim our goal.
The sacred bond that makes us free,
Is through His grace, our true decree.

Soaring Towards Tomorrow

On wings of faith, we lift our gaze,
To brighter paths, in hope's warm blaze.
Each dawn reveals a chance to grow,
In whispers soft, our spirits flow.

With every step, we leave the past,
Embrace the light, our shadows cast.
The sky awaits, a vast expanse,
In every chance, we choose to dance.

Guided by love, we find our way,
Through trials faced, we choose to stay.
With courage strong, our hearts ignite,
In unity, we craft our flight.

The stars align, as dreams unfold,
In every heart, a story told.
So let us soar, with spirits high,
In the embrace of endless sky.

Each moment treasured, hope's embrace,
Together we shall seek His grace.
With lift and joy, we rise anew,
For tomorrow waits, and we pursue.

The Crown of Resurrection

In whispers soft, the dawn does break,
A promise found, for all our sake.
From ashes rise, the spirit flies,
With every heart, the new day cries.

The crown of life, adorned with grace,
In faith we walk, we find our place.
Out of the tomb, the old departs,
And in its stead, a new light starts.

Through trials faced, we learn to see,
The higher callings set us free.
In love's embrace, we find our song,
With every note, we journey strong.

So let us bear the crown with pride,
In unity, we stand beside.
For in His name, we rise and bloom,
Through every shadow, we conquer gloom.

Rejoice, O souls, for we are whole,
In Christ's embrace, we find our goal.
With every breath, we raise the cry,
A testament that we can fly.

Beneath the Canopy of Hope

In stillness, faith takes root,
As whispers dance on gentle winds.
A promise cradled in each leaf,
Beneath the sky where love descends.

The branches stretch, in grace entwined,
Their shadows cast on weary hearts.
Each prayer a bloom in sacred ground,
Where spirit and the earth departs.

Hope flickers like a morning star,
Illuminating darkest night.
In burdens shared, our voices rise,
Together finding strength in light.

We walk the path of endless grace,
With every step, the soul's embrace.
The canopy, a shelter wide,
In unity, we bide our place.

So lift your eyes to heavens bright,
In every leaf, a hymn takes flight.
Beneath the canopy, we stand,
In love's embrace, hand in hand.

Fragrance of Newness

Awake to dawn's sweet serenade,
The earth adorned in morning dew.
With every breath, a spark is made,
In silence, old gives birth to new.

Petals unfold in colors bright,
Each blossom sings a sacred song.
In fragrant air, we find delight,
Where hearts and spirits both belong.

The sun breaks through the misty veil,
While shadows dance in fading night.
In every soul, a tale unveiled,
Of hope reborn in radiant light.

A symphony of life begins,
With laughter echoing through the trees.
In unity, the world spins,
Embracing all that brings us peace.

So lift your face to skies above,
Let newness wrap you like a shawl.
In every moment, feel the love,
For in this fragrance, we stand tall.

The Tides of Grace

Waves of mercy crash ashore,
Each ebb a promise, firm and sure.
With hearts attuned to nature's song,
In tides of grace, we all belong.

The ocean whispers tales of old,
Of journeys taken, dreams retold.
In every crest and every fall,
The rhythm calls, we heed the call.

With hands outstretched, we find our way,
Each grain of sand, a bright array.
Through tempest tossed, our faith renewed,
In salty tears, our hearts imbued.

So gather close, let spirits soar,
With open hearts, we'll seek the shore.
In unity, the waters flow,
As grace abounds, and love will grow.

For in the depths, a truth we find,
That every wave, a gift aligned.
Embracing life's vast, wondrous seas,
In tides of grace, we sail with ease.

Heavens Unfolding

Look upon the canvas wide,
Where stars above, in silence bide.
Each twinkle holds a whispered prayer,
In heavens unfolding everywhere.

The moonlight bathes the earth in glow,
A soothing balm for hearts that know.
In shadows deep, the light will play,
As night transforms to break of day.

Voices rise like ancient songs,
Through valleys deep and mountains strong.
In union, all creation sings,
Of love and peace that faith still brings.

Where clouds embrace the azure skies,
In every breath, a new surprise.
With every dawn, the promise clear,
In heavens unfolding, we draw near.

So raise your eyes, let spirits fly,
The sacred truths will never die.
In every heart, his love will dwell,
A story told, where all is well.

Chorus of the Renewed

In the stillness of dawn's light,
Hearts awaken, spirits take flight.
With chants of joy, we ascend,
In unity, our voices blend.

From ashes we rise, reborn anew,
Guided by faith, our souls pursue.
In sacred circles, love prevails,
Hope's gentle breeze fills our sails.

Through trials faced, we grow and learn,
In every corner, His light we yearn.
Hands joined together, we find our grace,
Embracing all, in love's warm embrace.

As mountains tremble, and rivers flow,
We stand with courage, hearts aglow.
His blessings rain down, pure and clear,
In every moment, He draws near.

In the chorus of life, we sing praise,
Finding strength in love's tender maze.
For from darkness, we boldly emerge,
With faith unfaltering, we rise and surge.

Graceful Resurgence

In twilight's glow, a whisper calls,
Awakening souls within ancient halls.
With each step forward, burdens we shed,
In the garden of faith, our spirits are fed.

The heartbeats sync with nature's pulse,
Drawing life from love, we feel the impulse.
As petals unfurl in softest grace,
We nurture the light in this sacred space.

Together we rise, hand in hand,
Building a bridge to the promised land.
Through valleys of shadow, we bravely tread,
With visions of glory, hope's light is spread.

In the symphony of all that's alive,
The warmth of our faith ignites and thrives.
Each moment a thread in the tapestry grand,
Woven by love, divine and unplanned.

So let every heart be open and free,
In the dance of creation, we find harmony.
As a graceful resurgence in truth we find,
The echoes of heaven forever entwined.

The Eternal Return

In the cycles of time, we find our way,
Through night and through dawn, we dance and sway.
The stars remind us of journeys past,
In sacred rhythm, we are steadfast.

From the depths of sorrow, we rise once more,
With faith as our compass, we open the door.
Every heartbeat whispers a holy decree,
In the light of His love, we are truly free.

Across the horizon, the sun will bestow,
A promise of hope in the afterglow.
As seasons change, so too shall we,
Embracing the path towards our destiny.

In the fabric of life, we're woven tight,
With each strand glimmering, pure and bright.
The eternal return, a circle unbroken,
In silence and prayer, our hearts have spoken.

And so we gather, all souls aligned,
In the gentle embrace of the divine.
For time is a spiral, a dance ever true,
In the heart of creation, we are made anew.

Breathe Life into Dreams

As dawn gives way to softest light,
Whispers of promise take their flight.
In the stillness, visions arise,
Carried by faith on wings to the skies.

With each breath drawn, a purpose ignites,
Lighting the path through darkest nights.
Embrace the journey, let worries depart,
For dreams are born from the depths of the heart.

In sacred spaces where silence sings,
We listen intently to what love brings.
Awaken the hopes held close to our soul,
As dreams unfold, we become whole.

Mountains may rise, rivers may swell,
But anchored in faith, all will be well.
Breathe life into visions, let courage grow,
In the garden of dreams, let the spirit flow.

With each cherished hope, we cast aside fear,
In the warmth of together, the path is clear.
So let us awaken, and endlessly strive,
For within us all, our dreams come alive.

Wings of the Sighing Heart

Upon the winds my heart does soar,
Carried by faith to a distant shore.
In quiet whispers, hope takes flight,
Guided by love through the darkest night.

Wings spread wide, my spirit calls,
In soft embrace, the soul enthralls.
Each sigh a prayer, each breath a song,
In the arms of grace, I will belong.

When shadows fall, I seek the light,
In trials faced, I find my might.
With every tear, a lesson learned,
In the heart's own flame, the spirit burned.

The journey long, the path unknown,
Yet with each step, love has grown.
In surrender sweet, I find my rest,
For in His arms, I am truly blessed.

So let me fly, with courage strong,
For in the heartache, I belong.
With wings of faith, I rise anew,
In the sighing heart, my spirit grew.

Redemption's Journey

In the valley deep, where shadows dwell,
A whisper calls, a silken bell.
With weary hands, I grasp the thread,
Of mercy's light, where hope is fed.

The path is steep, with stones of strife,
Yet each step leads to a new life.
Through trials faced and battles won,
In sight of dawn, the shadows run.

Wounds of the past, I lay to rest,
With faith in heart, I am truly blessed.
In the dance of grace, I find my way,
To brighter skies and a brand new day.

Redemption's song, a melody pure,
In every struggle, His love is sure.
With open arms, I seek the grace,
In every heart, I find my place.

So walk with me on this sacred road,
Where every burden becomes a load.
In the shadows cast, let light be found,
For in this journey, we are bound.

Together we'll soar, hearts intertwined,
In the love of the Divine, we are aligned.

The Glorious Rebirth

In the stillness of the morn,
A promise made, a heart reborn.
With every dawn, the shadows flee,
In golden rays, the spirit's free.

The past let go, the burdens light,
In love's embrace, the soul takes flight.
From ashes rise, the flame ignites,
In the depths of darkness, true love ignites.

New life awaits, in hope we trust,
With gentle hands, rebuild the dust.
Each beat a hymn, in gratitude sung,
In the song of life, we are young.

With every breath, new visions bloom,
A glorious dawn dispels the gloom.
In the tapestry of grace, we weave,
With every thread, we do believe.

So let the bells of joy resound,
In every heart, let love abound.
For in this rebirth, we find our way,
Together as one, come what may.

Awaken the spirit, embrace the light,
In the glorious rebirth, life is bright.

Echoes of the Divine

In the silence deep, a whisper calls,
Through sacred woods where the twilight falls.
With every echo, my heart shall glean,
The promises held in spaces unseen.

Reflections shimmer on the tranquil lake,
In gentle ripples, the spirit wakes.
Every leaf rustles a timeless tune,
Under the gaze of the watchful moon.

From mountain highs to valley lows,
In every heartbeat, the mystery flows.
In sun-kissed rays, the glory shines,
Through faith embraced, the soul unwinds.

With open arms, I reach above,
In the vastness known, I find His love.
The echoes whisper in breeze and dawn,
In every moment, I am reborn.

So let the songs of angels soar,
In every heart, we seek to implore.
For in the echoes of the Divine,
In every step, our spirits twine.

Together we'll walk, hand in hand,
In the embrace of grace, we will stand.

Divine Echoes of Revival

In the stillness of twilight's grace,
Whispers of hope, a sacred embrace.
Hearts awaken, the spirit finds light,
In the dance of shadows, darkness takes flight.

Through valleys low, where sorrows abide,
Faith blooms gently, the soul as a guide.
With every tear, a promise is sown,
In the garden of grace, we are never alone.

The warmth of deep love, it washes our fears,
In the river of mercy, we shed all our tears.
As dawn breaks forth, we rise to the call,
In our unity strong, together we stand tall.

Listen, dear wanderer, hear the refrain,
Hope sings sweetly, through joy and through pain.
With wings of forgiveness, we soar ever high,
In the chorus of life, we eternally fly.

So let us rejoice, in this sacred array,
With divine echoes, we find our way.
Revival within, a flame ever bright,
In the warmth of His love, we walk in the light.

Ocean of Forgiveness

In tides of mercy, our burdens we cast,
Waves of forgiveness, washing the past.
Hearts like vessels, drift upon seas,
In the cradle of love, we find our ease.

The shores of regret, we rise and we fall,
Yet the ocean's embrace, it beckons us all.
Grace flows like water, unbroken and free,
In the depths of His love, we find unity.

Each drop a promise, each swell a refrain,
The depths hold our shadows, and also our gain.
With every high tide, our spirits align,
In the ocean of life, the divine softly shines.

Let currents of kindness guide our way home,
In the vastness of mercy, we never roam alone.
Together we navigate, together we pray,
In the ocean of forgiveness, we find our way.

So breathe in the salt, let it cleanse your soul,
In this infinite sea, find healing and whole.
With faith as our anchor, we sail ever strong,
In the ocean of grace, may we always belong.

Sacred Seasons

In the springtime of faith, life blooms anew,
Petals of promise, kissed by the dew.
From the frost of despair, we rise from the ground,
In the cycles of time, His love knows no bounds.

Summer's embrace, warmth lighting our way,
Fields of devotion, where hopes gently sway.
With laughter in abundance, our spirits ignite,
As we gather in joy, hearts open and bright.

But autumn draws near, with whispers so wise,
The rustle of leaves, a beautiful sigh.
In the harvest of grace, we reflect and we share,
In the seasons of life, we find beauty in care.

As winter descends, cloaked in stillness deep,
In the quiet of waiting, our souls gently seep.
For in every season, His love is our guide,
With faith as our compass, in Him we confide.

So honor the cycles, the sacred divine,
In the dance of the seasons, His light brightly shines.
As we journey together, through every reprieve,
In the sacred of life, it's love that we weave.

The Promise of Spring

Awake, O heart, for the dawn draws near,
With petals unfurling, shedding all fear.
In the warmth of His light, new life is bestowed,
In the promise of spring, hope's story is sowed.

Mountains of doubt melt under the sun,
Rivers of joy flow, new journeys begun.
With each gentle breeze, whispers of grace,
In the arms of renewal, we find our place.

The chorus of birds fills the air with sweet song,
A symphony vibrant, where all souls belong.
With hearts intertwined, we rise and we sing,
For in every breath, there's hope that takes wing.

In gardens of faith, we plant seeds of love,
Tending to dreams, like stars up above.
As blossoms unfurl, we rise and we cling,
To the promise of spring, as new life takes wing.

So gather, dear souls, in this radiant hour,
In the fields of His grace, we flourish like flower.
With hearts open wide, let His light freely ring,
In the beauty of spring, let us joyfully sing.

Beyond the Veil

In shadows cast by holy light,
The spirits dance in sacred grace.
They whisper tales of endless night,
And promise hope, a warm embrace.

Beyond the veil, the truth does gleam,
A realm where love and peace reside.
We'll journey forth, entwined in dream,
As faith becomes our greatest guide.

The path is paved with tears and joy,
Each step a testament of trust.
In trials faced, no heart can cloy,
For mercy reigns and love is just.

We bow our heads and raise our hands,
To honor all that's pure and bright.
In unity, the heart expands,
We find our strength, our spirit's flight.

Beyond the veil, a world restored,
Where every soul shall find its song.
In harmony, we seek our Lord,
Together free, we all belong.

The Glory of Renewal

Awake, arise, the dawn is near,
The morning breaks with splendor's glow.
In whispers soft, our hearts sincere,
We greet the day, our spirits flow.

With each new breath, a chance to mend,
To cast aside all doubt and fear.
The past may fade, but love won't end,
In every moment, God is here.

Beneath the skies, our voices rise,
In praises sung, our souls take flight.
We seek the truth, the grandest prize,
In fields of grace, our hearts unite.

The glory shines through every tear,
In every loss, a chance to heal.
Renewed in faith, we persevere,
With every step, our hearts reveal.

As petals bloom, we find our place,
In sacred trust, we lift our eyes.
The glory of renewal's grace,
Awaits the soul that seeks the skies.

Covenant with the Sun

The morning's light, a pledge divine,
A covenant with day begun.
In golden rays, our souls align,
With every rise of faithful sun.

The warmth it brings, a gentle guide,
Through shadows deep, we'll find our way.
With open hearts, we turn the tide,
Embracing love, come what may.

Each dawn a gift, each dusk a prayer,
In nature's arms, we find our home.
With gratitude, we breathe the air,
And seek the paths where saints have roamed.

As twilight falls, we reflect and gaze,
Upon the stars, a sacred trust.
In every moment, love's bright blaze,
Shall lead us on, it is a must.

Our covenant sealed with every dawn,
In harmony, we rise and run.
With hearts aglow, we carry on,
Forever bound, a gift, the sun.

Surging Faith

Like rivers flow, our faith does surge,
With currents strong, it sweeps us near.
In storms of doubt, we feel the urge,
To cling to hope, to persevere.

Each wave that breaks upon the shore,
Reminds us of our sacred vow.
In trials faced, we're called for more,
To rise again, to humbly bow.

Through valleys deep and mountains high,
We venture forth with spirits bold.
With trust in hand, our eyes on sky,
We seek the light, the truth untold.

The heart ignites with every prayer,
A flame that burns, a guiding star.
In every challenge, love laid bare,
Our surging faith will carry far.

So let us walk with heads held high,
In unity, we'll journey forth.
In every laugh, in every sigh,
We'll share the blessings of our worth.

Awakened Souls

In the quiet of dawn, we find our way,
Whispers of hope lead us to stay.
Hearts open wide, embracing the light,
Awakened spirits, taking flight.

With each breath, we rise above,
Bound by faith, wrapped in love.
Together we walk, hand in hand,
Discovering truth in a sacred land.

The shadows fade, the darkness clears,
In the grace of God, we cast our fears.
Every step is a dance, divine,
Awakened souls, forever shine.

In the stillness, we hear the call,
A gentle reminder, we are not small.
Carried by faith, held by grace,
In this journey, we find our place.

With eyes wide open, we see the thread,
Connecting all hearts, our spirits led.
Together we rise, united and free,
Awakened souls, in harmony.

Illuminated Paths

In the glow of the evening star,
We walk the path from near to far.
Guided by love, our hearts aflame,
Illuminated paths call each name.

Through valleys deep and mountains high,
We search for truth, we question why.
With every step, we find our way,
In the light of faith, we choose to stay.

The gentle breeze carries our prayers,
A symphony of hope, lifting cares.
Hand in hand, we journey forth,
Illuminated paths, revealing worth.

Each dawn brings new beginnings clear,
A promise held, forever near.
In the embrace of joy, we tread,
Illuminated paths where angels led.

In unity, we forge ahead,
By love's sweet whisper, we are fed.
Through trials faced, our spirits soar,
Illuminated paths forevermore.

The Promise of Tomorrow

Each sunrise brings a brand new chance,
In the light of hope, we find our dance.
With faith as our anchor, strong and true,
The promise of tomorrow, guiding you.

Through storms that rage, we hold our ground,
In the darkest nights, love will be found.
Every tear we shed, a seed of grace,
The promise of tomorrow, in time and space.

With every heartbeat, a story unfolds,
Courage ignites, as destiny holds.
We walk in trust, embracing each new day,
The promise of tomorrow, lighting the way.

When shadows loom and doubts arise,
Remember the light that never dies.
In every moment, find peace and calm,
The promise of tomorrow, a healing balm.

Together we rise, hand in hand,
In the grace of love, we make a stand.
With hope leading us, dreams will grow,
The promise of tomorrow, forever aglow.

In the Embrace of Grace

In the silence of night, we seek the light,
In the embrace of grace, all feels right.
With gentle whispers, the spirit does speak,
In every moment, it's strength we seek.

Through trials faced, we rise anew,
With hearts united, we pursue.
In each challenge, we find our song,
In the embrace of grace, we all belong.

Tender mercies, like rain from above,
Nourishing souls with abundant love.
In the vastness, we feel His embrace,
In the embrace of grace, we find our place.

With arms open wide, we gather near,
In the warmth of faith, we cast our fear.
Together we journey, steadfast and brave,
In the embrace of grace, we learn to save.

Forever forward, our spirits soar,
In the embrace of grace, forevermore.
With love as our guide, we trust and believe,
In the embrace of grace, we learn to receive.

In the Footsteps of Angels

In the whispers of the night,
Heavenly beings take their flight.
Guiding souls through shadows deep,
In their embrace, we softly sleep.

With wings adorned in light so bright,
They lead us forward, hearts alight.
Each step we take, their grace we feel,
In faith, our wounds they gently heal.

Through trials vast and tempests wild,
They walk with us, a loving child.
In every tear and every smile,
Their presence rests, divine and mild.

The path to peace, they softly show,
With every sign, our spirits grow.
In the footprints left on dust,
We find the strength to rise and trust.

So lift your eyes, behold their light,
For in their care, we find our fight.
With angels near, we shall not fear,
In sacred vows, our hearts draw near.

Miracles in the Darkness

In shadows deep, the heart does yearn,
For flickering lights, as candles burn.
In silence, hope begins to bloom,
A gentle grace dispels the gloom.

Each prayer whispered, softly sent,
A guiding force, divinely lent.
From ashes rise the brightest flames,
In trials faced, we call their names.

The night may seem a daunting foe,
Yet in its depths, our spirits grow.
For darkness fades with every dawn,
And in that light, our fears are gone.

With every tear, we learn to see,
The hidden joy, the path to free.
In brokenness, our strength is found,
As miracles in silence sound.

So stand with grace through every storm,
For in His love, we are reborn.
With eyes wide open to the skies,
In miracles, our spirit flies.

Voices of the Reborn

In echoes soft, the past does call,
A melody of hope for all.
Through trials faced and battles fought,
A symphony of love is wrought.

In every heart, a story waits,
From brokenness, new life creates.
With voices raised, we sing our praise,
To Him who guides us through our days.

The chains of doubt, they fall away,
As night gives way to risen day.
With every breath, our spirits soar,
For in His light, we've found much more.

The whispers of the once forlorn,
Now sing aloud, and we are reborn.
In unity, we find our song,
Together in this place, we belong.

So gather close, and hear the tune,
For hope is found beneath the moon.
In voices strong, we hold the key,
To everlasting joy and glee.

Eternal Call to Hope

In every heartbeat, hope resounds,
Through trials faced, true strength abounds.
With every dawn, a promise made,
In love and light, our fears allayed.

The road may wind, and shadows loom,
Yet faith ignites a flower's bloom.
In darkest nights, we hear the song,
A call to rise, where we belong.

With open hearts and hands held wide,
We walk together, side by side.
In every challenge, we embrace,
The light that shines from His own grace.

Through whispers low and voices high,
The spirit lifts, we learn to fly.
With every step, we seek the sun,
In hope eternal, we are one.

So take my hand, let faith ignite,
For love will guide us through the night.
In unity, we find the way,
An eternal call for every day.

Divine Embrace

In shadows cast by fading light,
We seek Your warmth, O Holy Might.
With every breath, we call Your name,
In quiet storms, we find the same.

Your grace like rivers gently flows,
Through barren lands, where true hope grows.
In every heart, a sacred plea,
To dwell within, O God, with Thee.

Upon the altar, fears release,
The weight of sin gives way to peace.
With lifted hands, we trust, we stand,
Forever held in Your own hand.

In whispered hymns, our spirits soar,
To realms beyond, forevermore.
Each trial faced, a step towards Light,
In love's embrace, we take our flight.

Embrace us, Father, in Your grace,
Let us behold Your blessed face.
In every tear, Your love we trace,
Awakening in warm embrace.

Whispers of Salvation

A gentle breeze brings forth Your voice,
In broken hearts, You make us rejoice.
Through darkest nights, we heed Your call,
In faith we rise, and shall not fall.

Your light reflects on waters deep,
In troubled souls, Your promise keep.
Each tear we shed, a sacred trust,
In You alone, we place our thrust.

The path You chart is paved with gold,
In every story, love unfolds.
Embraced by arms, unseen yet near,
In silence sweet, Your voice we hear.

We wander wide, yet find our way,
In every dawn, a brand-new day.
Your whispers guide through stormy test,
In You, O Lord, we find our rest.

With humbled hearts, we seek to know,
In every seed of faith, You sow.
Let grace abound, and love increase,
In whispers sweet, grant us our peace.

Vows of the Heart

In covenants made, our spirits bind,
To You, O Lord, our hearts aligned.
Through trials faced and dreams we pursue,
Our vows remain forever true.

With earnest faith, we take our stand,
Two souls united, hand in hand.
In life's embrace, we'll find our grace,
With every step, we seek Your face.

When storms arise, and shadows fall,
In sacred trust, we heed Your call.
Together bound, through thick and thin,
In You, dear Lord, our lives begin.

Our voices lifted, hymns resound,
In sacred moments, love is found.
Through joy and pain, we journey on,
In every hymn, our hearts are drawn.

So let us vow, and let it be,
In faith and love, we shall be free.
With hearts ablaze, eternally,
Together rise in harmony.

Celestial Climb

Upon the peak of heaven's grace,
We strive to see Your holy face.
With every step, our spirits yearn,
In sacred fires, our hearts now burn.

The stars above like lanterns bright,
Illuminate the path of light.
With faith as wings, our course we steer,
In trials faced, we draw You near.

The mountain speaks, in silence deep,
Of promises that You will keep.
In every trial, a lesson learned,
In every heart, Your love returned.

Through valleys low, and heights so grand,
We walk with courage, hand in hand.
For every dream that's yet to come,
In You we stand, our hearts become.

So lead us, Lord, to heights sublime,
In faith we glow, our spirits climb.
In every breath, Your love we find,
Celestial grace within our minds.

Transformation in Faith

In shadows deep, the heart does yearn,
To seek the light, for truth we burn.
Awake, O spirit, rise and soar,
Embrace the love that's at your door.

With gentle hands, the Savior greets,
In every trial, His grace repeats.
A whisper soft, a guiding hand,
Through faith we walk, together stand.

The path of doubt begins to fade,
As trust in Him our fears invade.
In every prayer, our souls align,
In sacred peace, His love divine.

With every breath, a promise made,
Through stormy seas, we are not swayed.
For in His name, we find our might,
In darkness, He becomes our light.

As blossoms bloom, we are renewed,
In faith's embrace, our hearts are stewed.
Together bound, in hope we thrive,
In transformation, we come alive.

Holy Reawakening

Awake, my soul, and rise anew,
In holy grace, the morning hue.
The dawn is here, with whispers kind,
In every heart, His love we find.

With open arms, the heavens sing,
A melody of hope they bring.
In sacred dance, our spirits sway,
To lead us on this blessed way.

The waters flow, a cleansing stream,
In faith we find our truest dream.
Each drop of mercy falls like rain,
In grateful hearts, we cast our pain.

The angels gather, singing clear,
Their voices whisper, "Do not fear."
In unity, we stand as one,
In holy light, the battle's won.

A sacred flame within ignites,
Through darkest nights, He guides our flights.
With joy we rise, our burdens shed,
In holy reawakening, we're led.

Hopes Rejuvenated

In dreams of old, our hopes take flight,
With every dawn, brought forth by light.
In joy, we find what's long denied,
In faith and love, we turn the tide.

Each tear we shed, a seed is sown,
From brokenness, a garden grown.
In trials faced, our strength is found,
Through darkest storms, His love surrounds.

With open hearts, we seek the grace,
A holy path, our saving place.
In fellowship, we lift each other,
Through trials shared, we find a brother.

As mountains rise, our spirits climb,
In every moment, love transcends time.
Through struggles met, our hopes revived,
In faith's embrace, we come alive.

In vibrant hues, the world transformed,
With every prayer, our hearts are warmed.
Together strong, we rise and sing,
With hope renewed, our spirits spring.

Everlasting Embrace

In quiet moments, love is found,
In every heartbeat, grace abounds.
Eternal arms, they hold us tight,
In endless love, we find our light.

The promise made, forever sure,
In faith we stand, our hearts endure.
Through every trial, every storm,
In His embrace, we are reborn.

With every breath, a song of praise,
To guide us through these winding ways.
In unity, our spirits soar,
In sacred space, we long for more.

As seasons change, His love remains,
In every joy, in all our pains.
A bond that time cannot erase,
We find our peace in His embrace.

Together bound, through all of time,
In every moment, love's pure rhyme.
In everlasting, we find our home,
In joyful hearts, we are not alone.

Reborn in Faith

In the silence of the night, my heart awakes,
Whispers of the divine, gentle as the lake.
I rise from the ashes, reborn anew,
With faith as my guide, I embrace the true.

Hands raised in surrender, I seek the light,
Every burden lifted, darkness takes flight.
In grace I believe, on paths yet untrod,
My spirit ascends, embraced by my God.

A chorus of angels sings deep in my soul,
Within every heartbeat, I feel the whole.
Through trials and triumphs, I walk the path,
In love's warm embrace, I find my true wrath.

Cleansed by the waters, I start to renew,
With each drop of mercy, my heart finds its cue.
In unity gathered, we rise as one,
Together in faith, the journey's begun.

Every step a prayer, each breath a hymn,
In the light of His love, our hope will not dim.
The journey is sacred, our souls intertwine,
Reborn in this faith, forever I shine.

The Ascending Spirit

In the dawn of creation, where dreams take flight,
The spirit rises high, journeying toward light.
Guided by the stars that shimmer on high,
With each whispered prayer, my soul learns to fly.

Through valleys of shadows, I wander in grace,
Seeking the truth in this vast, holy space.
Each step a reminder of the path I tread,
With love as my anchor, I follow ahead.

Voices of the ancients echo in my heart,
Their wisdom ignites the divine spark.
Awakened to purpose, I soar on the breeze,
The spirit ascends with such effortless ease.

In the warmth of the sun, my spirit will dance,
Embracing the moment, lost in its trance.
Every breath, a promise, each sigh, a song,
In this sacred journey, I know I belong.

An orchestra of angels plays sweet melodies,
Their harmonies guide me, setting my spirit free.
With faith as my compass, I seek and I find,
The ascending spirit, forever aligned.

Anointed by Sunlight

Morning breaks softly, with rays of pure gold,
Anointing the earth with blessings untold.
Each beam a reminder that hope is alive,
In the warmth of the sunlight, my spirit will thrive.

The flowers awaken, their petals unfurl,
In the dance of creation, a wondrous swirl.
With whispers of beauty that speak to my soul,
Together in worship, we become truly whole.

In moments of stillness, I bask in the glow,
Each flicker of light a profound way to grow.
The sunlight, a symbol of grace that I seek,
Illuminating paths that once felt so bleak.

I gather the blessings, I gather the dreams,
Believing in miracles, bursting at the seams.
In this realm of wonder, my heart learns to sing,
Anointed by sunlight, I embrace everything.

As the day gently fades, I'm bathed in the dusk,
A promise of twilight, in faith I can trust.
With each soft transition, I hum with delight,
Anointed forever, by the love of the light.

Transcending Shadows

In the depths of silence, where shadows reside,
I search for the light that can never subside.
With courage, I venture, beyond what I know,
Transcending the darkness, I choose to let go.

Each fear I release, like leaves from a tree,
In the embrace of the light, I long to be free.
The echoes of doubt, they fade in the night,
As wisdom and hope guide my soul to its height.

Moments of stillness, where whispers ignite,
The flame of the spirit, a beacon of light.
In the warmth of connection, we rise hand in hand,
Transcending the shadows, united we stand.

With prayers like arrows, we shoot for the stars,
In the battle of life, we carry no scars.
For every dark moment is followed by dawn,
A promise of healing, a journey reborn.

With faith as our armor, we break every chain,
Transcending the shadows, refusing the pain.
In the dance of existence, our spirits set free,
In the light of redemption, we finally see.

New Beginnings

In the dawn's gentle light, we rise,
With hope in our hearts, we claim the skies.
The past fades away, like mist in the air,
A new path unfolds, our burdens laid bare.

Each step that we take, guided by grace,
In faith we move forth, each trial we face.
The promise of life, renewed every day,
In love's warm embrace, we find our way.

Through shadows and storms, we journey on,
In whispers of peace, despair is gone.
With eyes open wide, we see the light,
In the arms of the dawn, all wrongs made right.

The seed of our dreams, planted with care,
Blossoms in joy, fragrant in the air.
With courage we stand, as the sun appears,
In the newness of life, we cast aside fears.

Together we sing, our voices unite,
In harmony found, with all of our might.
For every new start, a blessing bestowed,
In the garden of hope, our spirits are sowed.

Ageless Truths

In whispers of time, the sage will speak,
Of love everlasting, the strong and the meek.
The heart knows the way, through valleys of doubt,
Through trials endured, we rise and shout.

The stars bear witness, the moon lights the path,
In silence we learn of divine aftermath.
Each truth leads us home, a beacon of grace,
A journey of souls, in this sacred space.

The rivers that flow, with wisdom they bear,
Remind us of mercy, of answered prayer.
With faith as our compass, we traverse the deep,
The ageless truths of love, our hearts always keep.

Through stories we share, the lessons unfold,
In tender embrace, brave hearts can be bold.
For in every moment, the spirit renews,
The ageless truths shine, where love always woo.

So let us remember, through laughter and tears,
The strength of the past, conquering our fears.
In unity bound, we rise and we dance,
In the light of the truth, we seize every chance.

In the Wake of Resurrection

From darkness to light, the stone rolled away,
Hope springs eternal, in this new day.
With joy overflowing, we celebrate life,
In the wake of the dawn, all sorrow seems rife.

The spirit ignites, with flames ever bright,
In hearts rekindled, we bask in the light.
Each moment a gift, in love we believe,
In the wake of resurrection, we rise and we grieve.

In fragile hearts, the echoes of grace,
Remind us of joys, though we've known our place.
For loss is but part of the journey we take,
In the wake of resurrection, our souls shall awake.

With hands open wide, we embrace the new day,
In faith we walk forth, in love we will stay.
For every ending holds promise anew,
In the wake of resurrection, our hearts will renew.

So sing out the truth, and dance in delight,
For the gift of this moment shines brightly at night.
With grace as our guide, we are never alone,
In the wake of resurrection, we find our true home.

A Symphony of New Life

In melodies sweet, nature sings her song,
In harmony's grace, we find where we belong.
The whispers of spring, a promise divine,
A symphony plays, where our souls intertwine.

The blossoms awaken, their colors so bright,
Each petal reveals, the beauty of light.
In every heartbeat, the rhythm resounds,
A symphony of life, in love, we are found.

With every sweet note, our spirits arise,
In joyous refrain, our troubles subside.
Through valleys of doubt, we dance and we sway,
A symphony echoes, lighting the way.

In laughter shared loud, and in whispers so soft,
We weave our connections, lifting hearts aloft.
For in the together, our strength we will find,
A symphony of new life, forever entwined.

So let us rejoice, as the music unfolds,
In gratitude's chorus, our story is told.
With love as the anchor, our souls will unite,
In a symphony of life, we embrace the light.

Celestial Awakening

As the dawn breaks forth, the heavens align,
In celestial embrace, our spirits entwine.
The stars whisper secrets, as night gives way,
To the breath of new life, that greets the day.

In stillness we gather, our hearts open wide,
In the dance of creation, we stand side by side.
The cosmos is singing, with love as the key,
A celestial awakening, setting us free.

With grace in our steps, we traverse the skies,
In the warmth of the sun, our burdens will rise.
The beauty of moments, in each fleeting breath,
In celestial awakening, we embrace life and death.

Each dawn is a canvas, painted anew,
With colors of hope, in every hue.
In the embrace of the stars, our souls shall ignite,
In celestial awakening, we dance with delight.

So let every heartbeat, echo the song,
Of love everlasting, where all hearts belong.
In unity found, we rise ever blessed,
In celestial awakening, our spirits find rest.

Seraphic Restoration

In the light where angels dwell,
Hearts are mended, fears dispel.
Whispers flow from sacred streams,
Restoration in divine dreams.

With every tear that falls like dew,
Hope ignites a vibrant hue.
From ashes rise, the soul ascends,
In grace, the journey never ends.

The wings of faith will guide our way,
Through the night to break of day.
Together, in love we stand tall,
In unity, we heed the call.

As the seraphim sing above,
We embrace the purest love.
In the stillness, peace descends,
Restoration that never bends.

Let our spirits intertwine,
In the grace of the divine.
With every step, we seek the light,
In the bonds of joy, unite.

Graceful Rebirth

From the shadows, dawn does break,
In the silence, a heart awakes.
New beginnings, softly spoken,
In the love, all chains are broken.

Every journey leads us home,
In the grace, no need to roam.
Through the trials, lessons learned,
In our souls, the fire burned.

Spirit whispers, guiding true,
In the depths, we find the view.
Wrapped in mercy, we are whole,
In the light, we find our role.

Grace flows gently like a stream,
In our hearts, it plants a dream.
With each breath, we rise anew,
In the path of faith, pursue.

Through the struggle, we will soar,
In the rebirth, seek for more.
With open arms, the world awaits,
In the grace, our spirit states.

Echoes of the Redeemed

In the stillness, voices rise,
Echoes heard beneath the skies.
From the depths of pain and strife,
Redemption gifts a brand new life.

Bound in hope, together we sing,
Of the joy this love can bring.
Chains of doubt begin to fall,
In the light, we hear the call.

Every heartbeat, a sacred trust,
In the ashes, find the dust.
From despair, our spirits flee,
In the echoes, we are free.

Journey forth with open hearts,
In the truth, each part imparts.
With our voices, we align,
In the grace, forever shine.

Through the trials, hope remains,
In the love, we break our chains.
With the echoes, rise and soar,
In redemption, evermore.

Wings of the Spirit

Lifted high on wings of grace,
In the spirit, find our place.
Through the trials, joy will guide,
In the love, we take our stride.

With each moment, nurture light,
In the darkness, be the bright.
Let the faith be our refrain,
Wings of spirit break the chain.

In the beauty of the dawn,
Hope awakens, fears are gone.
Guided by the sacred muse,
In the flight, our hearts we choose.

Every heartbeat, chant in time,
In the rhythm, love will climb.
Through the valleys and the heights,
On the wings, we reach new sights.

Trust in whispers of the wind,
In the spirit, we descend.
With our souls unbound and free,
Wings of grace, our destiny.

United, we shall rise and fly,
In the love, we touch the sky.
With the spirit, we will soar,
Guided by the unseen shore.